Math = Fun!™

Count
by
Fives

by Jerry Pallotta
Illustrated by Rob Bolster

SCHOLASTIC INC.

New York   Toronto   London   Auckland   Sydney
Mexico City   New Delhi   Hong Kong   Buenos Aires

Welcome Kirill and Anna Mastrocola!
— *Jerry Pallotta*

For children who play in sandboxes and dream of someday operating full-sized equipment.
— *Rob Bolster*

ISBN-13: 978-0-545-00245-5
ISBN-10: 0-545-00245-1

12 11 10 9 8 7 6 5 4 3 2 1   8 9 10 11 12 13/0

Printed in the U.S.A.
This edition first printing, January 2008

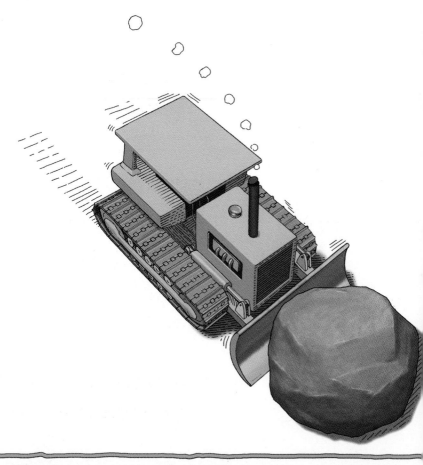

Welcome to the construction site.
It is time to get to work.

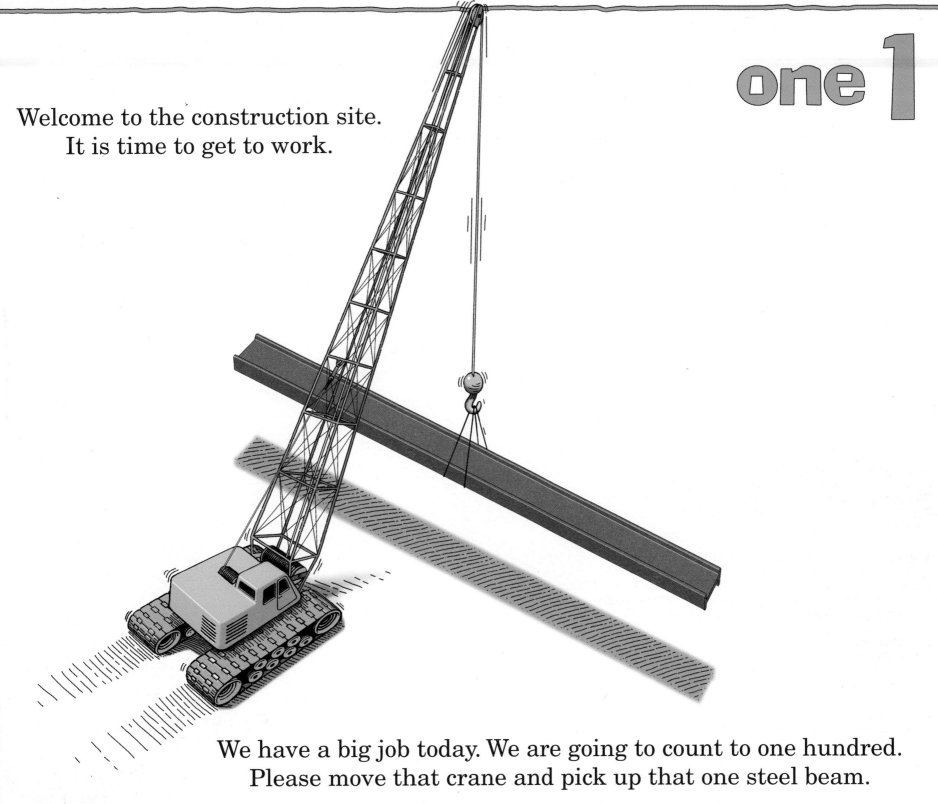

We have a big job today. We are going to count to one hundred.
Please move that crane and pick up that one steel beam.

2 two

Before we count to one hundred by fives, we are going to count to ten.
The backhoe can pick up these two piles of gravel
with either its front bucket or its back bucket.

Here comes the bulldozer. Keep on moving the three boulders.
We wish they were diamonds and rubies but they are granite.

4 four

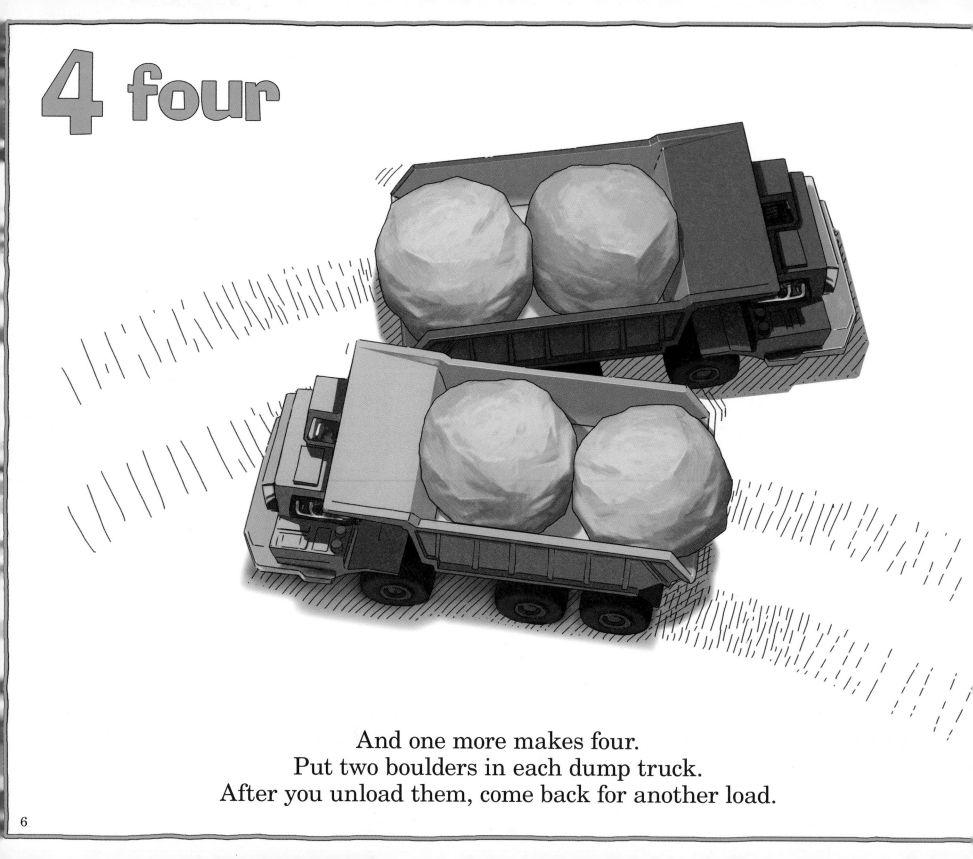

And one more makes four.
Put two boulders in each dump truck.
After you unload them, come back for another load.

Beep. Beep. Beep. Beep. Watch out!
That forklift might back up at any time.
Be careful while those five gears are being lifted. Don't run over the pallets.

6 six

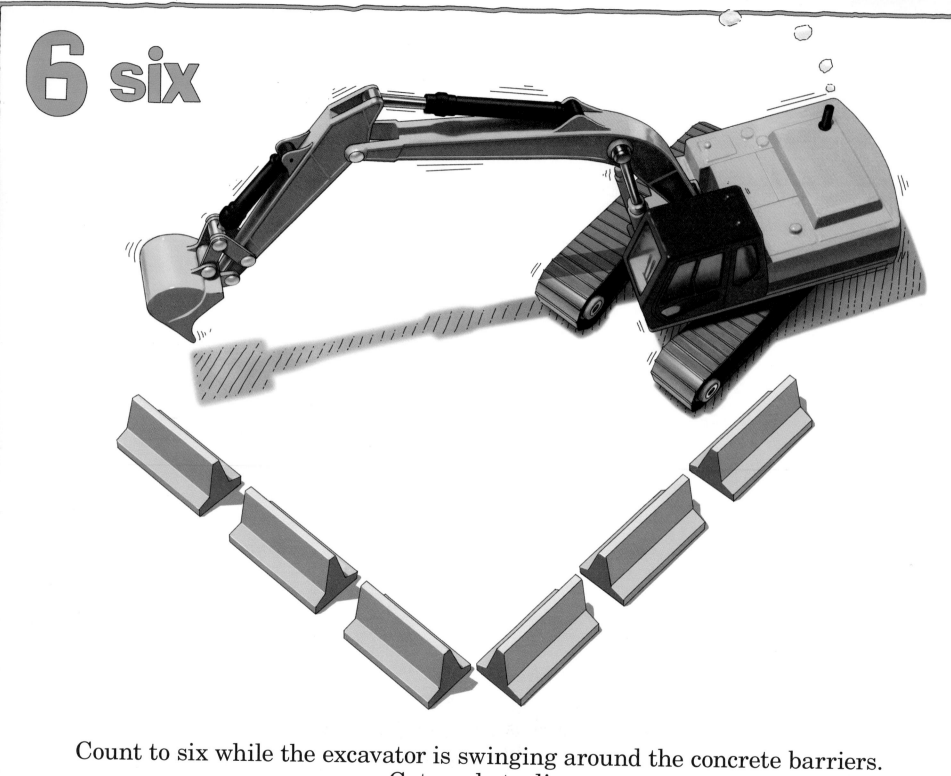

Count to six while the excavator is swinging around the concrete barriers.
Get ready to dig.

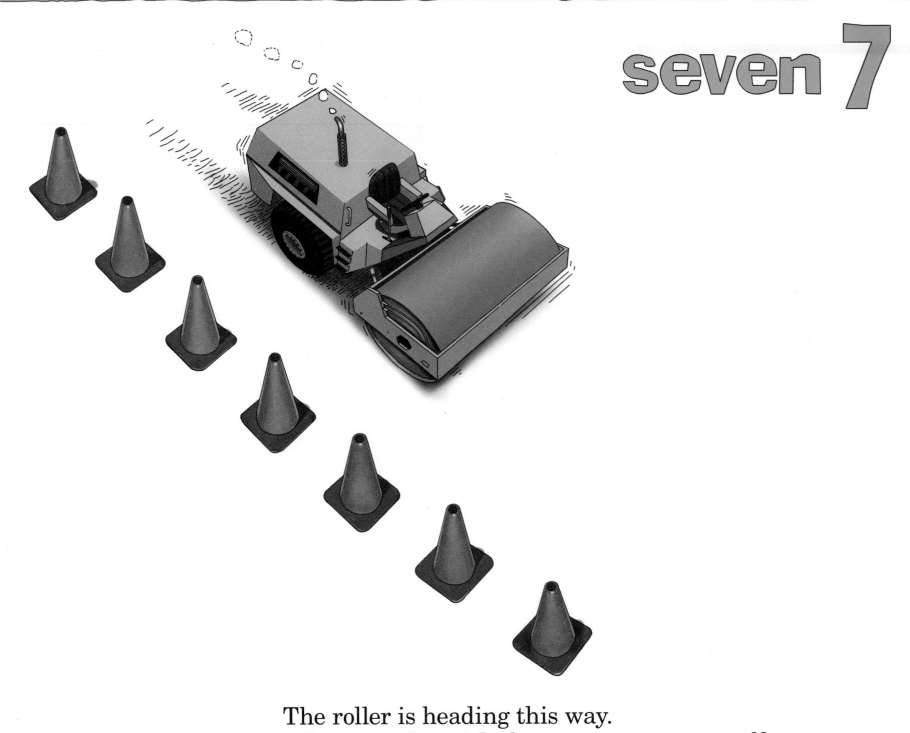

The roller is heading this way.
Let's hope it does not roll over and squish these seven orange traffic cones.

8 eight

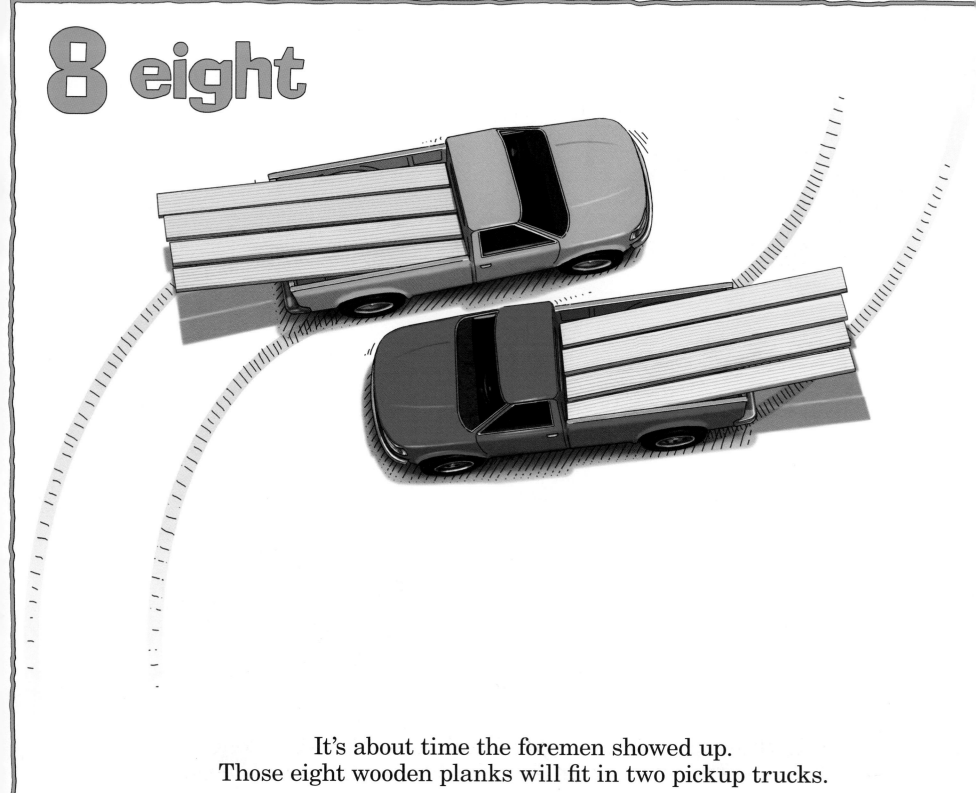

It's about time the foremen showed up.
Those eight wooden planks will fit in two pickup trucks.

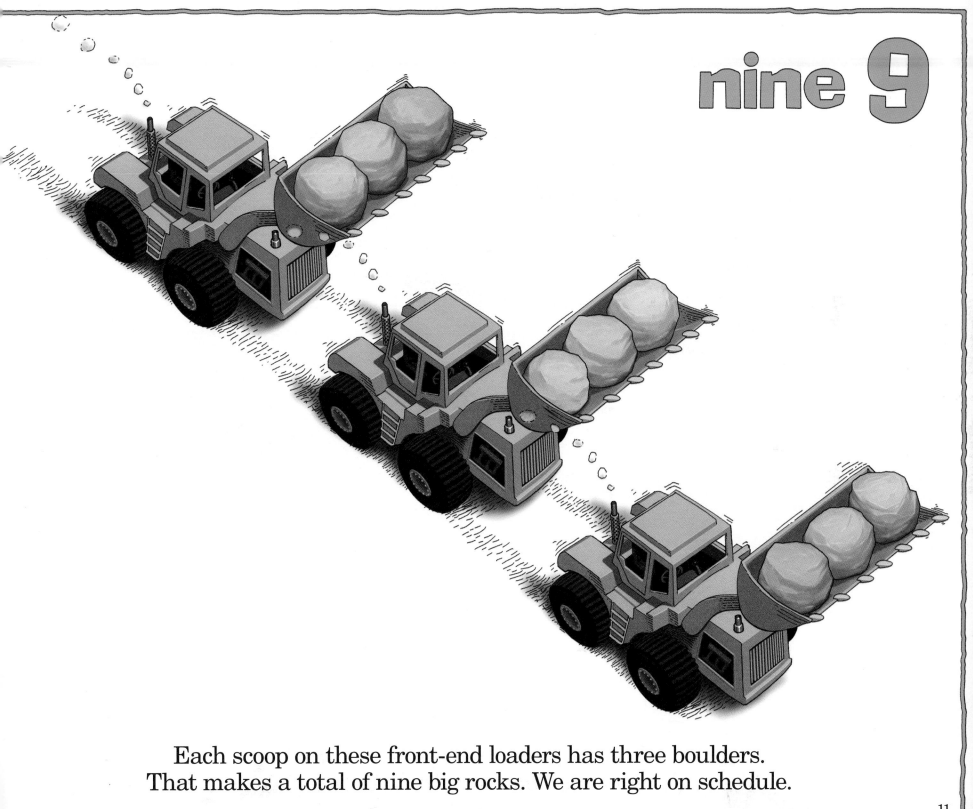

Each scoop on these front-end loaders has three boulders.
That makes a total of nine big rocks. We are right on schedule.

10 ten

We need to load ten steel beams on this flatbed eighteen-wheeler.
Oh, no! Someone forgot to load them.
We counted to ten by ones, now we are going to count to one hundred by fives.
Five, ten, and we keep on going!

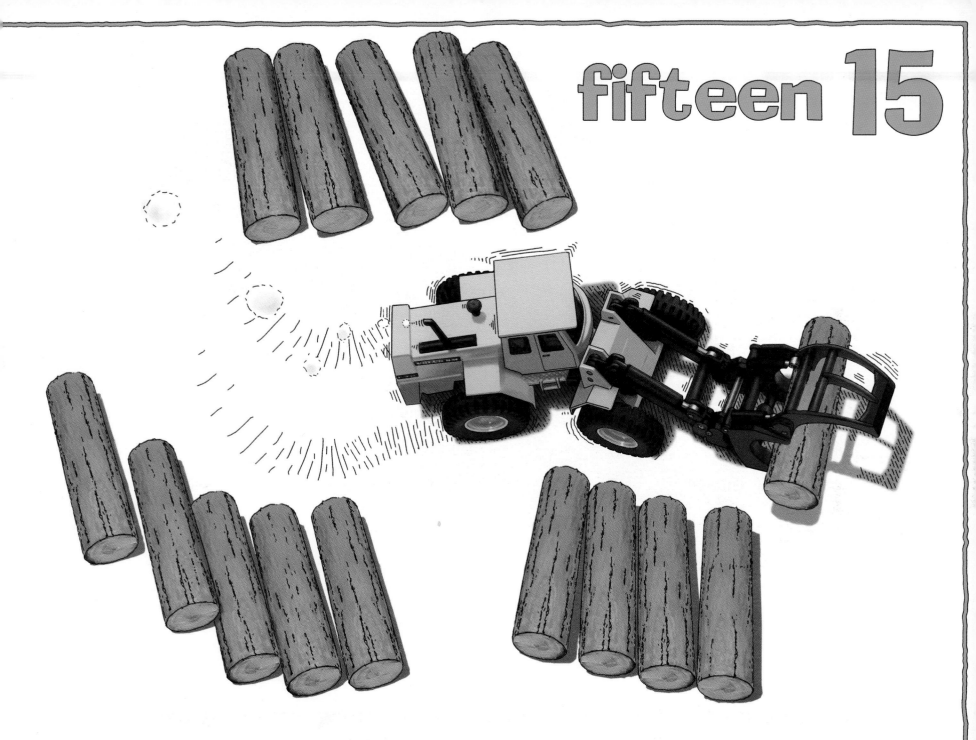

Here is a grapple. A grapple is perfect for picking up logs.
Let's put the logs in sets of five each. Five, ten, fifteen.

20 twenty

Here are twenty cinder blocks.
The Bobcats can turn in a complete circle if it will help.

We usually use this rack truck to carry tools,
but today we are moving twenty-five orange traffic cones.

30 thirty

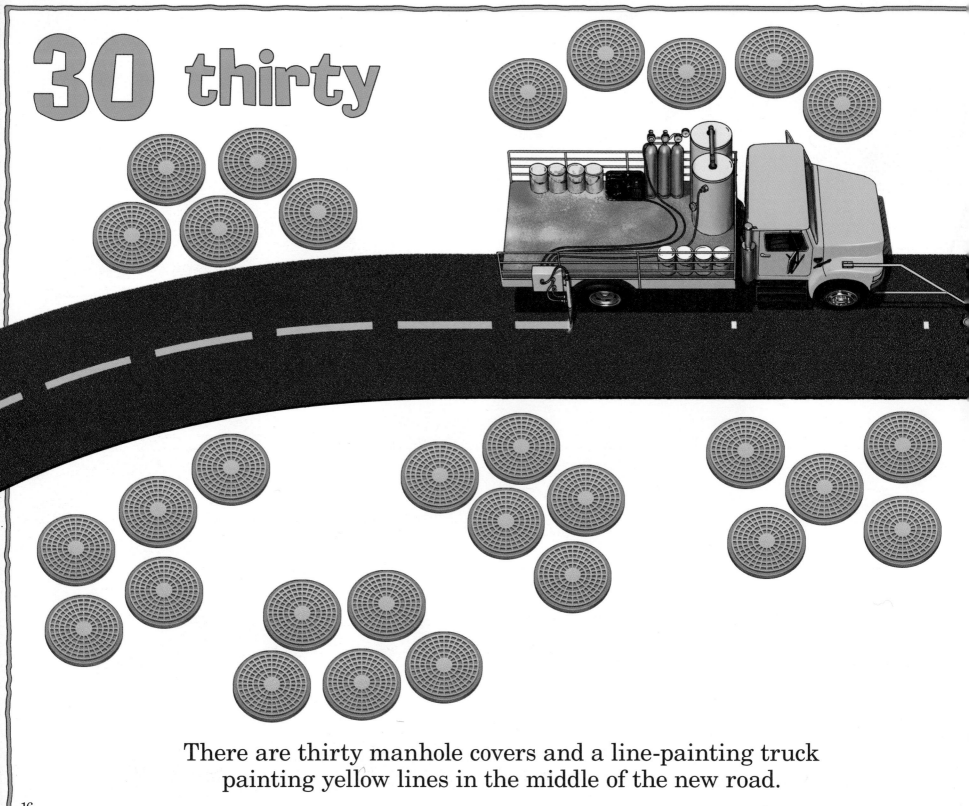

There are thirty manhole covers and a line-painting truck painting yellow lines in the middle of the new road.

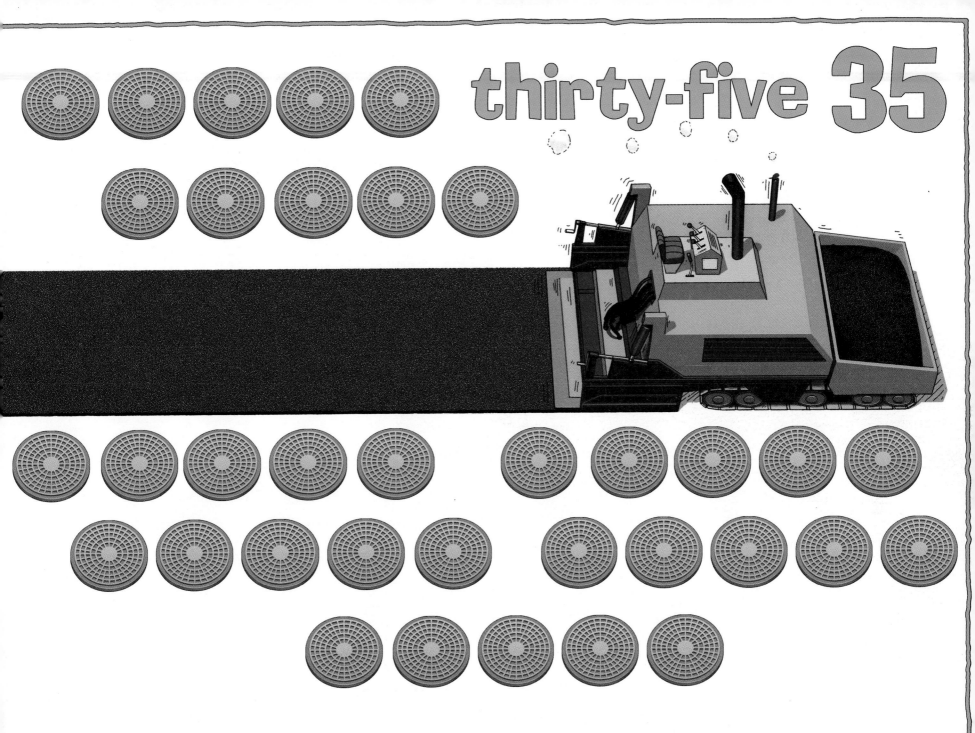

The road paver is laying the asphalt.
Count another thirty-five manhole covers as the road is being built.

40 forty

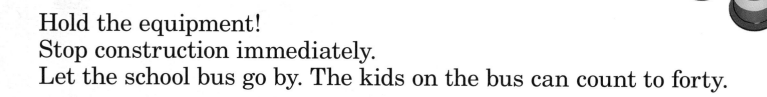

Hold the equipment!
Stop construction immediately.
Let the school bus go by. The kids on the bus can count to forty.

It is cleanup time.
Let the street sweeper drive between
the forty-five traffic barrels.

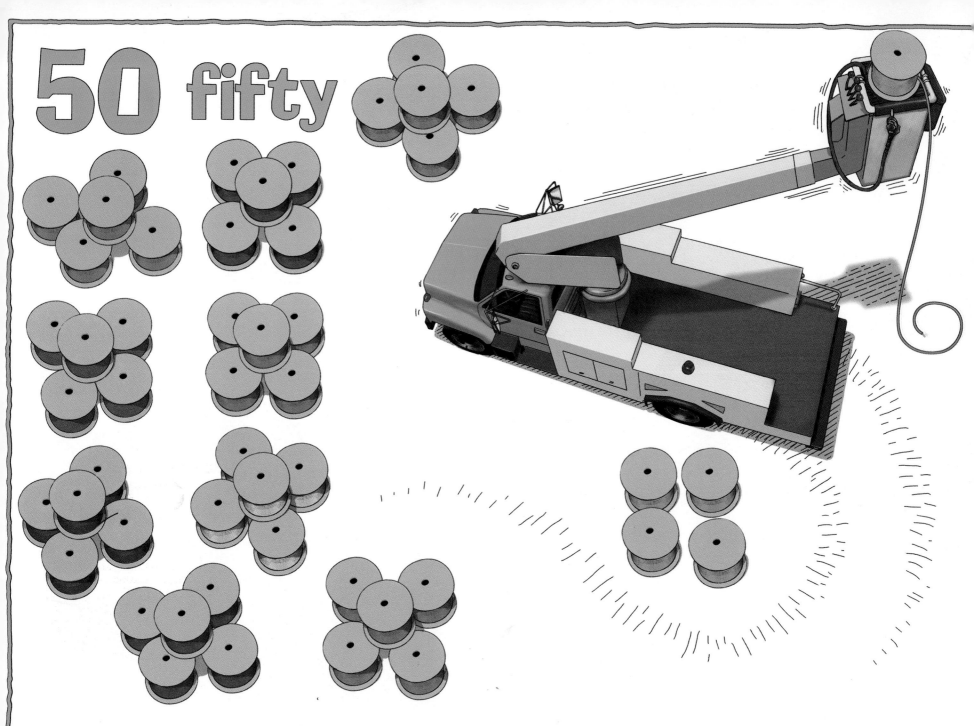

50 fifty

Here are forty-nine cable spools plus one in the bucket of the cherry picker.
Hooray, that makes fifty cable spools!
We are halfway to one hundred. The job is looking good.

The cherry picker broke down. We need a tow truck.
We are at fifty-five and counting!

60 sixty

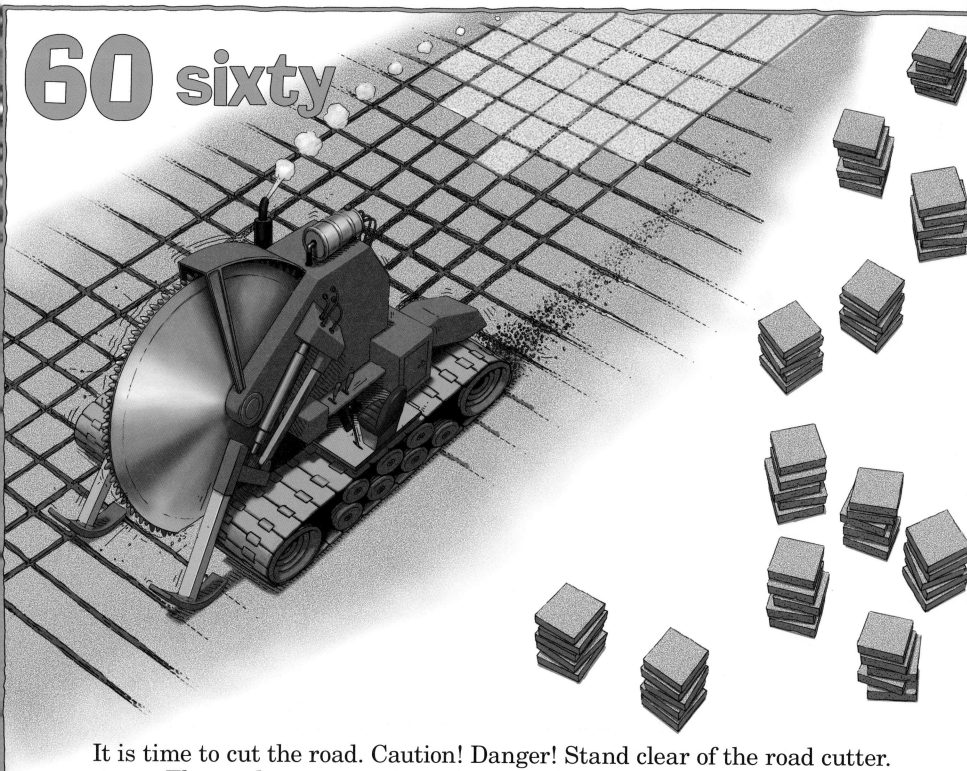

It is time to cut the road. Caution! Danger! Stand clear of the road cutter.
The road cutter is loud, but we can still count sixty squares.

Here is a scissor lift going up, up, up as we count up, up, up to sixty-five bricks.
Five, ten, fifteen, twenty, twenty-five, thirty, thirty-five,
forty, forty-five, fifty, fifty-five, sixty, sixty-five.

70 seventy

The tanker truck arrives next.
Count the seventy water jugs and then fill the jugs on the pickup.
The pickup truck will bring the water to the job site.

seventy-five 75

It looks like the cement mixer holds seventy-five concrete piles. Perfect! We are three-quarters of the way to one hundred.

80 eighty

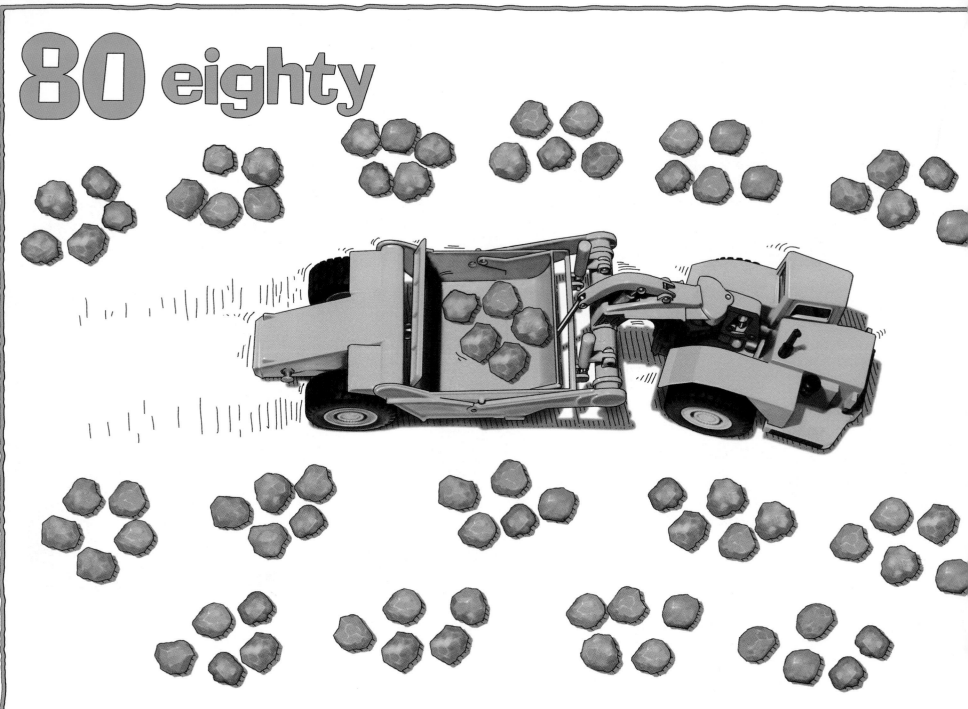

This strange-looking vehicle is a scraper.
It can scrape up or unload dirt. There are eighty rocks on this page.
Don't forget to count the five rocks that are in the scraper.

Here comes the grader right through the eighty-five concrete pipes.
In wintertime, the grader can plow snow.

90 ninety

An auger is used to drill holes.
Count the ninety holes while you are watching the auger drill into the ground.

Here comes a race car! Don't count too fast or you will get a speeding ticket.
Ninety-five traffic cones do not mean ninety-five miles per hour.

one hundred

We made it all the way to one hundred.
The conveyor belts help.
Five, ten, fifteen, twenty, twenty-five, thirty,
thirty-five, forty, forty-five, and fifty.

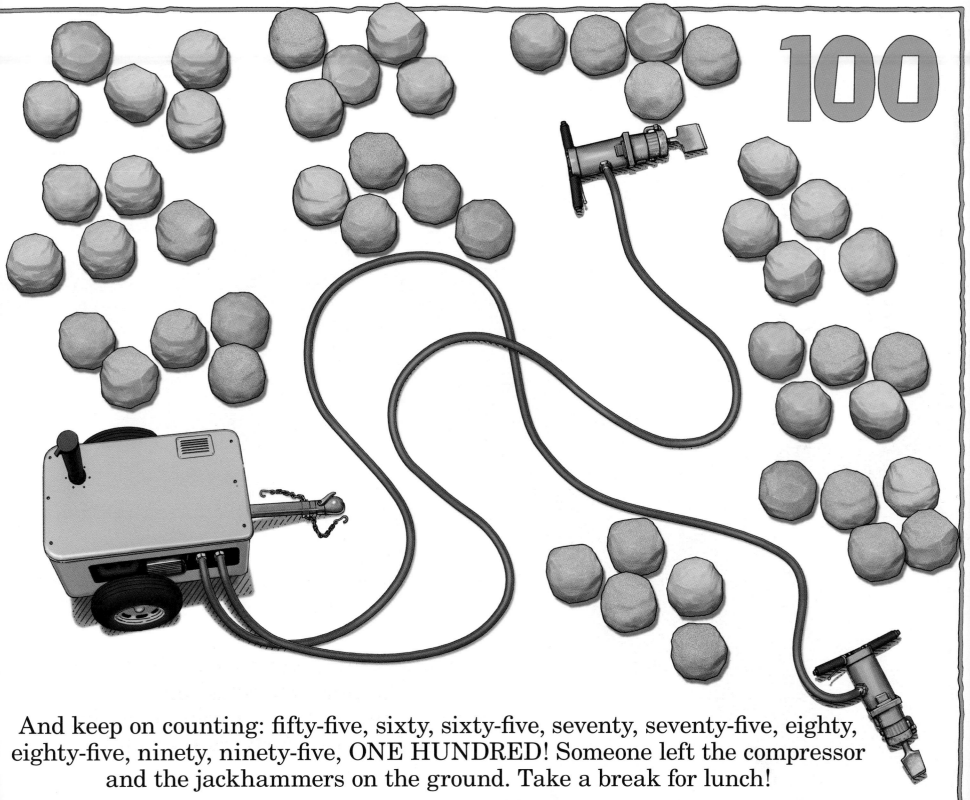

And keep on counting: fifty-five, sixty, sixty-five, seventy, seventy-five, eighty, eighty-five, ninety, ninety-five, ONE HUNDRED! Someone left the compressor and the jackhammers on the ground. Take a break for lunch!

0 zero

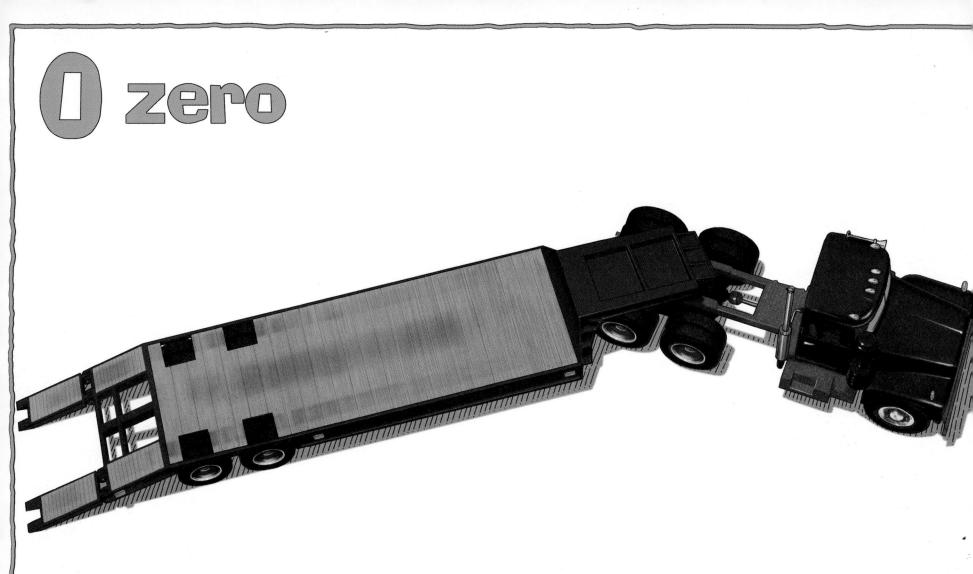

Everyone is at lunch.
There is nothing to count. Zero.
The low bed trailer is here to pick up the construction equipment
and bring it to another job site.
Zero has been loaded. But a lot has been learned!
Math equals fun when you count by fives!